OUT OF THE SHED
DELUXE EDITION

Roger Penwill
2017

OUT OF THE SHED – deluxe edition.

First Printing: 2017

ISBN: 978-0-244-02279-2

Penwill Cartoons
Ludlow, Shropshire UK

www.penwillcartoons.com

Printed by lulu.com.

Other books by Roger Penwill:

Cartoon Aided Design
Cue Pixels – Action!
Assembled Cartoons
The Countryside Cartoon Joke Book
Layers? - What Layers?

OUT OF THE SHED
DELUXE EDITION

GREAT FORGOTTEN MOTORCYCLE PROJECTS

Roger Penwill

Dedicated to Finley and Lois.

INTRODUCTION

Despite its title, this book is not about sheds. In fact sheds don't feature in it at all. So all you dedicated shed enthusiasts out there you've bought the wrong book; it's not for you. Nothing to see here. Move along.

The connection with sheds is that this is a book about things that were built in sheds in the 1940s to 1960s...big sheds, small sheds, even medium-sized sheds. Wooden sheds, concret block sheds, wriggly tin sheds, corregated asbestos sheds.....

And it's not just about any old things built in sheds. Specifically it's about motorbikes and even more specifically about things production motorbikes were made into, in sheds.... Motorbike projects that created road machines that pragmatically fulfilled all sorts of essential tasks, with varying degrees of success, or not.

These heroic projects often went unnoticed, which was a pity. Well, now they have been noticed and here they are, celebrated in this volume.

Please note that projects built in garages are not included, for obvious reasons.

If you have been an avid reader of the Classic Bike Guide in times past, you may have seen already these projects, because that's where they have been shown before.

However, the vast extra space available for this collection allows for a more in-depth and detailed description of each project.

If you should happen by some strange chance to see one of these on the road please notify me immediately. It means it hasn't actually been forgotten and therefore should be deleted from future editions.

Roger Penwill

About this Deluxe Edition

It's in colour!

About Roger Penwill

He is someone who knows very little about motorbikes.

THE PROJECTS

The Green Sidehouse

Launched in 1953, the year of Queen Elizabeth's coronation, to coincide with that great event and also the conquest of Everest, Herbert Winciette Wynes conceived and built the first Green Sidehouse.

It was a delight for the dedicated motorculturalist who felt the need to tend his petunias on the road. He, and others of similar ilk, mostly felt that need near Slough, although it could be cured by medication.

Somewhere between the growing season and Friday afternoon rush-hour, the rider was advised to be in low pootle gear with the sun on the right. To achieve germination it was then necessary to travel in light rain after sunset.

Although several of these sidehouses were built, an invasive snail problem caused speed issues with the bike performance. Despite installing bird houses in later models to counteract the snails, the problem persisted and Mr Wynes gave up. No further green sidehouses were built.

He rented a nine-inch telly instead.

The Green Sidehouse

The Vincent Potter

This was one of only two models developed by the renowned pot-thrower Nicholas "Crisps" Bitsprangler-Wilson, which were devised for the Cornish mobile fast ceramics industry.

Typically a customer would send a telegram requesting a new pot to Mr Bitsprangler-Wilson . Upon receipt, he would drop everything to attend to the new order. This resulted in many broken pots and a team of under-potters (or *sous poteurs* in Cornish) were employed to invisibly mend them.

Meanwhile, Mr Bitsprangler-Wilson, keen to eagerly fulfil the fast ceramics order, would leap onto the Vincent Potter and in a loud voice demand that the bike take him to the client. On most occasions the bike didn't go anywhere. Sometimes it fell over.

Despite a vari-speed potters wheel, an on-board firing oven, both powered by the work-horse 998cc Vincent-HRD Rapide vee-twin, and functional offset clay panniers, the Potter was not a success. This was mainly because Mr Bitsprangler-Wilson didn't really understand motorbikes. At all.

Today Bitsprangler-Wilson invisibly-mended pots are still collected. This is so they can be properly disposed of.

The Vincent Potter

The Sunbeam C-Front

Enormously popular from Scarborough to Skegness during the holiday camp hey-day of the Fifties, the C-Front was widely modified and personalised by more than three of its owners. One was even seen in Clacton.

This gang of C-Fronters would descend on a seaside resort, dressed in their distinctive striped one-piece leather bathing suits and knotted handkerchief protective headgear.

They would ride menacingly slowly long the esplanade, stopping to openly chew candyfloss, drink tea and buy postcards. Such was their reputation that many tea rooms refused to serve them knickerbocker glories.

The legendary "Lido" model with its distinctive aroma of chlorine and it's wooden modesty panels, not seen here, was also not seen anywhere else either.

The Sunbeam C-Front

The Norton 99 Cocoon

Possibly designed to appeal to the countryside rider, the 99 Cocoon was a masterpiece of understated woven wattling. It was an early example of rural aerodynamics, effortlessly blending with passing hedgerows and local washer-women heading to the river with their laundry.

The real purpose of the Cocoon and why it was built is a little unclear. It is also not known who actually built them.

Mostly they were found abandoned in country lanes in Wiltshire.

They are believed to have been evolved from unpowered bicycle versions that were commonly found abandoned in country lanes in Wiltshire several years before.

The motorbike version nevertheless is regarded as an unsurpassed manifestation of two-wheeled all-weather high speed basketry.

Except in Wiltshire, where it was just a nuisance.

The Norton 99 Cocoon

The Douglas MkIII Sport Inn

This was one of the many bikebars, or motopubs, popular in the Fifties and Sixties before the arrival of the police Drunkanovathelimitmeter in 1967 curtailed drinking and riding.

Bikebars were owned and staffed by the proprietor who most often would be an ex-World War II fighter pilot called Algernon. The older, more established motopubs, were owned by ex-World War I fighter pilots also called Algernon

These road-side, or ditch, hostelries were common sights on arterial road lay-bys. Even short road journeys were long in those days, so frequent refreshment stops were needed. If necessary, drinks could be served on the move as the motopub was ridden alongside traffic. This involved reaching out a pint to a car or lorry driver, a manoeuvre known as a "stretch of road".

The landlord of the particular motopub shown here was Group Captain Algernon "Squiffy" Barnes-Bridge, formerly of Triple X Squadron. He called time for the last time in 1972.

The Douglas MkIII Sport Inn

The Ariel Scout Leader Camper

Dean Bigglesworth, tent development manager and scouting person in the Rickmansworth and Surrounding Areas Division of the Young Chaps Brigade, was a keen advocate of the travel tent.

His concept took the the joys of camping on the road. Whilst on the move, you could do absolutely everything you would want to do in a tent.   Except sleep, which was tricky, if not impossible.

The Scout Leader Camper could accommodate two, one lying on top the other.   This was only recommended for friends.

It was difficult to keep the parafin stove lit as the airflow tended to blow out the flame. It also stopped the kettle boiling.

It never quite took off to achieve the iconic status the camper van enjoyed. It did, however, take-off - far too frequently in a following wind.

The Ariel Scout Leader Camper

The AJS Model 16 Robinetta

This blend of the 3-wheeled car and motorcycle was a successful, if short-lived, experiment in the late Sixties. It had the discomfort of such a very small car combined with the ride-ability and instability of a bike. The least-best of both worlds.

This particular model could have been the inspiration behind John Lennon's infamous psychedelic Rolls Royce livery, but probably not.

The Robinetta was slightly ahead of the wave of the Flower Power movement and may even have helped generate it. It was centainly popular with hippies. One such attempted to ride it naked from Bexleyheath to the Woodstock Festival. He got as far as Catford.

The AJS Model 16 Robinetta

The AJS Model 16 (1947) Camperette

A two-wheeled precursor of the camper van, these AJS variants were known originally as Low Overhead Camperettes the, more commonly, L.O. Campers.

They were particularly popular with globe-trotting Antipodeans who would buy them in England for the Grand Tour of Europe and sell them on their return. They were a common sight outside the Kafe Kwik-Kipfen on the Hamburg autobahn.

When the outriggers were retracted for travel, it was necessary for fellow camperette riders had to run alongside holding it upright until it reached at least 20mph for stability and they could let go.

The AJS Model 16 Camperette

The 1958 Aermacchi Chimera Calda Aerea

Continuing the combined traditions of Italian aviation and motorcycling, Umberto Nutella di Deeti of Verona developed the personal dirigible (i.e. steerable) hot-air airship.

Lift was provided by the bike exhaust gases and forward propulsion by revolving paddles attached to the rear wheel. When not in the air, it would simply revert back to being a motorbike. It took just two days to convert the vehicle from one form to the other.

When being a motorbike it needed a lorry to follow behind with the envelope, semi-rigid keel, rigging, paddles, gas flue, pipework and Italian flag. When being an airship, an 8-man ground handling crew in two support vehicles was required.

Until his accident, Nutella maintained that the view from the air made it all worthwhile.

The Aermacchi Chimera Calda Aerea

The Mark I 1950 Dotlitzer Blackpool

Adapted from the Dot Milk Float 3-wheeler, which was the rear half of a Dot motorcycle with a modified front end, the Dotlizer incorporated a stereo keyboard sound system that was revolutionary for the time.

The latter was a highly tuned narrow gauge Wurlitzer compatible, modelled on the organ of the Blackpool Tower ballroom.

A prototype Mark II was planned, which allowed the front end to rise out of the ground while the rider played quickstep favourites and the occasional waltz. However the project was abandoned when it was realised it would involve digging large holes in the road.

The Mark I Dotlitzer Blackpool

The Vincent "Grey Flash Rocket" 500cc

Between 1949 and 1952 just 31 thoroughbred Vincent Grey Flash variants were made. This was the not-so-thoroughbred 32nd.

The revolutionary personal aerodynamic rider capsule produced a top speed just slightly slower than the non-Rocket models.

The Grey Flash required a raked launch block and a corresponding landing block at journey's end to load and decant the rider respectively. This need for landing blocks inevitably limited the choice of places it could be ridden to.

It was an interesting and innovative concept that proved problematic.*

*It didn't work.

The Vincent "Grey Flash Rocket"

The Triumph 3TA All-Weatherer

Built in 1962, the All-Weatherer featured a sturdy climate-protective upper body in the distinctive and iconic inverted bath tub style.

This was particularly popular in Welsh mining villages as the top could be detached in well under three hours and used as a family bath tub. Not only could the All-Weather keep water off on the road but also keep it in when off.

In forward motion, the top did tend to collect significant mud from the road and after long journeys the rider would have to be dug out.

The Triumph 3TA All Weatherer

The BSA Bantam Eggsycle

In the early 1950's, the Bantam Eggsycle was as common a sight on town streets as the R White's lemonade lorry or rag-and-bone men on a horse and cart yelling "Olragsunlumber!!".

The National Administrative Board For The Marketing, Distribution And Selling Of Jolly Good Eggs (or the NABFTMDASOJGE for short) commissioned and subsidised a national fleet of Eggsycles to deliver fresh eggs and chicken manure to town dwellers.

Many can still recall with affection their weekly arrival on the suburban street accompanied by the happy sound of clucking, the rider's loud cry of "Eggsunmuck" and a pungent aroma down wind.

The Eggsycle became redundant after the arrival of the self-powered mobile battery hen which meant that hens could go free-lance, cutting out the middle-man.

The BSA Bantam Eggsycle

The Jawa Mekke Jizda

This distinctive machine was devised in Czechoslovakia in 1957. This 250cc 2-stroke variant utilised the rubberised fabric Li-Lo technology so popular on the beaches of Europe at that time.

Although "mekke jizda" translates as "soft ride" the bounce effect when fully inflated earned it the nickname "The Prague Spring". The up-down motion made people feel sick.

It was also involved in countless accidents as it was near impossible to ride, but, on the plus side, riders were seldom harmed. For this reason it is seen as the precursor of the airbag, which can commonly be found in present day automobiles if you crash the car hard enough.

The Jawa Mekke Jizda

The 1952 Royal Enfield Flying Flea

Because of its light weight, which gave it its name, this Royal Enfield was suitable for dropping by parachute and landing anywhere remote, rugged, inaccessible and probably wrong.   To get it to the correct drop zone it was also designed to be carried over rough terrain that would otherwise be unpleasant to carry a bike over, even in nice weather.

By the early 1950's mountaineers had adapted the typical 1944 protective frame to make it easier to carry the bike over Everest and similar peaks. Some cheated by having the bike dropped by parachute on the top of the mountain. Gravity would then assist the bike-carriers descent to base camp and even beyond, depending on when they could reach the brakes.

The wartime, but still functional, built-in parachute was retained in case a high peak should happen to be fallen off. At lower levels, the bike could quickly be dismantled and released from the frame when flat bits of land were encountered.

They could go back later to collect the frame.

The Royal Enfield Flying Flea

The 1963 Norton Blue Boxette

Paired to a Norton Commando, this side car was a essentially a mobile constabulary moderate response unit. It was first trialed in the Home Counties at the police mobile moderate response unit test and dog track near Tring.

The police boxette unit had a reputation of being much smaller on the inside than it looked from the outside. This greatly restricted effective truncheon movement and its application therein.

Miscreants taken "down the Nick" had to be strapped to the roof. This was difficult to achieve securely because of the blue lamp and, at speed, some offenders were accidentally released early without charge.

The Blue Boxette featured in many famous Ealing comedy films, perhaps the most well-known being the Blue Lamp Belles of Pimlico Mob.

The Norton Blue Boxette

The Ducati Gran Sport Cornetto

In the highly competitive world of ice cream selling in the 1950's this Italian-built sports vendorette was unbeatable.

In the daily race to reach the prime selling location alongside a beach or popular sand dune, the Ducati Cornetto was always there first. It was parked with the refrigerator fired up and pumping out coldness a long time before any native British-built ice-cream tricycles arrived and started stacking their cornets.

The Cornetto had the additional advantage that the public, and AA patrolmen, could buy ice cream before it melted and dripped down their trousers.

The Ducati Gran Sport Cornetto

The 1950 Excelsior Talispostman

This swift 244cc bike saw much service as a two person workhorse for the General Post Office combined post and delivery operation.

A front-facing postal operative would handle collection and delivery of items, whilst a rear-facing operative would deal with letter-sorting and providing cups of tea.

Few such bikes were actually seen on the roads of Great Britain as the movement of mail took place at in the dark at night when the bike's lights became ineffective.

The infamous Great Motorbike Robbery happened in 1952 when 23 guineas in unmarked postal orders were dumped on a yew hedge by the road and the bike purloined.

The Excelsior Talispostman

The 1966 Matchless Mobile Public Bathhouse

The Matchless G80CS was a powerful, tough, no-nonsense, off-road model which proved to be perfect for reaching and providing a stimulating cold bathhouse facility for Yorkshire miners in the 1960's.

Keen for their dinner, miners could bathe as they rode back from the pit, to be clean and fresh by the time they arrived home to the wife and her steaming dumplings.

In the morning's ride to work they bathed in the previous night's water. This was deemed necessary to reapply the regulation soot and grime before reaching the pit.

The Matchless Mobile Public Bathhouse

The 1959 Honda Super Hero Manga Cub C100

In 1959, Mr Eric Winkle constructed this variation on the Honda Super Cub to transform it and himself into a Japanese style fantasy robot. He integrated the metal head helmet, gloves and boots into the bike structure.

To provide a suitable feng-shui environment to construct his bike he constructed and then adapted a unique pagoda shed near Nuneaton.

Powered by a super-powerful 50cc 4-stroke engine this bike inspired the famous iconic "You Meet The Nicest Robots on a Honda" marketing campaign.

The Honda Super Hero Manga Cub C100

The Triumph Thunderbird Six
Eagle Hide

Developed for the American market in the 1960's in Evesham, this hide (or rapid avian spotterbox to give it it's correct title) was the brain child of Ms Marion Nation, founder of the UK Chapter of Hell's Ornithologists. It was a common sight on commons, especially in long grass.

Specifically the hide was aerodynamically designed to spot American Bald Eagles and then to chase and peruse them at great speed to study closely their social, hunting and shopping habits.

Ms Nation's choice of the Triumph Thunderbird proved to be inspired, but only two hides survived the ensuing eagle attacks.

The Triumph Thunderbird Six Eagle Hide

The Douglas Dragonfly Moto-Angler

The Douglas Dragonfly motorbike was produced from 1953 until 1956. This variation of it was for touring urban anglers who didn't have time to sit beside rivers, canals, streams, brooks and the like to do their fishing.

It was powered by a whisper-quiet 348cc horizontally-opposed twin-cylinder four-stroke engine universally recognised for not scaring the fish.

The attractive design won the Moto-Angler Gazette's Best Pike Bike Award for one year in succession. Although it had a large-capacity fish tank, onboard fly-catcher and optional dragnet, the Moto-Angler had poor brakes and a low cruising speed. Low speed meant the bike wobbled and spilled the water.

These problems made it unpopular with its owner. A comprehensive survey of the owners established that there was only one of them – Mr Dennis Klot of Shenfield East.

The Douglas Dragonfly Moto-Angler

The 1957 Matchless G80 Assize

Throughout the late Fifties, High Court touring judges would take their sessions at weekends in country fields around hilly and often muddy courses.

These "circuit" judges would hold competitive trials, seeking a conviction of the accused within five laps in a clockwise direction. Appeals were dealt with in the final event of the meeting.

Pictured is the notoriously strict Judge Race Reece-Tart, known as the Pranging Judge.

When races took place in foggy weather he often declared them to be "mist trials".

The Matchless G80 Assize

The 1962 Ariel Arrow Old Chapper

During the Sixties, retired motorcycle enthusiasts descended en mass on towns like Frinton and St. Leonards in their "Chapper" bikes. These were modified, tuned-down Ariel Arrows with on-board front lawns and occasional herbaceous borders.

Sometimes as many as six formed a local "Chap-ter", often having heated disputes with neighbouring Chap-ters over issues like the names of garden butterflies and the height of hedges.

Gnomes were not allowed.

The most notorious of these late-lifers was Herbert "Leafy" Laine, pictured above, who was known for his violent and extreme patience, especially in pension queues. Local people would talk of being intimidated by his politeness.

The Ariel Arrow Old Chapper

The 1962 Francis-Barnett Fulmarbar

After Vince Thunder's rock 'n' roll career ended at the start of the 1960's he decided to open a coffee shop for his rocker mates to chill out in. He opened it in Basildon. It failed.

He then decided it had to be mobile, so it could fail in other places too.

Adapting an Francis-Barnett Fulmarbar, he added a coffee percolator and a pair of matching juke-boxes. The latter machines could play the same record at more or less the same time, creating what Vince called "Paireo" sound.

By then stereo had been invented so no-one was interested.

It still failed. Everywhere.

The Francis-Barnett Fulmarbar

The BSA M21 Breakdown Bike

When the Automobile Association stopped using its motorcycle patrols in 1961 it sold off all its BSA M21 motorcycle combinations, after rubbing off the AA logos.

Several people, including Mr William Sparg-Russett, purchased one of them and set themselves up as rivals to the A.A. Mr Sparg-Russett began the Breakdown Bike (BB) service, equipping the side car with an abundance of spare car parts.

Aware that the public missed being saluted by the AA motorcycle patrolmen, he installed a rubberised fabric arm, inflated via an on-bike air scoop. The air doubled as a store of air for flat tyres.

The BSA M21 Breakdown Bike

The 1950s BMW "Harmony"

Towards the end of the 1950's several touring choirs turned to using bike and sidecar combinations to perform concerts on the road, bringing quality singing to accompany and serenade late afternoon and evening traffic.

These passing renditions were very popular before the age of decent car radios.

The particular choir shown here is the West Ealing Male Moto-Ensemble.

Actually built from three separate BMW motorbikes, the resulting BMW variant was known as the Three Part Harmony.

The BMW "Harmony"

The Sunbeam S8 Thatchback

From the start of the 1950's there was a great resurgence of Morris Dancing among rural middle-aged men with beards. They formed themselves into Clog Chapters, travelling to public houses on modified Sunbeam bikes.

The most notorious clog gang was the East Herefordshire and District Red Barellers, seen here in its entirety, who used Sunbeam S8s.

Their bitter rivals were the Worcester Double Diamonds, who rode S7s. Wild Stick dance clashes between the groups left many Morris Men bloodied, hungover and needing a drink.

The Sunbeam S8 Thatchback

The 1959 Ducati 125 UFO Sport

Many people believed in the late Fifties that Earth would soon be invaded by aliens from another planet, most probably Mars.

Amateur UFO spotters began to hold night-time vigils, watching for alien space craft. Mobile saucer receptacles were built, based on this typical Ducati model, designed to race speedily to the latest UFO hotspot.

Each of these was developed in line with accepted interplanetary alien proportions. In the spirit of getting along with aliens, it therefore provided any accosted extra-terrestrial with a bed, desk, nice curtains and a glass of water.

The Ducati 125 UFO Sport

The 1956 James Cadet L15 One-man Deep Water Bell

These diving bells were a common sight on the south coast of England in the late 1950's. Inspired by the underwater TV documentaries, they were assembled on 147cc James bikes.

After being ridden down to the shore-line, the bell's telescopic legs were lowered to the sand and the bike detached.   The mechanical legs of the diving bell and the human legs of the rider-diver were next retracted into the craft and the flaps closed.

The bell was then rolled on its out-riggers into the sea, pushed by any sun-bathers available on the beach. The Water Bells only worked on deeply shelving beaches, or, to facilitate exploration at a greater depth, by being pushed off a cliff.

The James Cadet L15 One-Man Deep Water Bell

The 1965 Velocette Venom

A sight often seen on the beach at Paignton was the strangely hypnotic snake-driving by what appeared to be an authentic Indian fakir.

It was, in fact, a Mr Stanley Legges of Torquay, who had the amazing ability to charm a cobra to steer his sand-Velocette as he played an authentic Indian mouth flute whilst seated on a saddle of nails.

Usually the snake, whose name has been lost, completely failed to turn the front wheel in the sand and the bike would slowly keel over. The snake then would quickly escape and would be captured by members of the local beach rounders team.

Eventually Mr Legges decided that the snake would have be replaced. He bought a second-hand anaconda, but it was too large for the front basket and was also tone-deaf. He swapped that for a Python who was found later to prefer traditional jazz and a good knees-up.

The Velocette Venom

The 1965 Triumph T120R Bonneville Three

The 650 twin was used for this slightly challenging three-wheeler. It could speedily convert from a powered conventional motorbike to a free-wheeling unpowered "coaster" down hills, thus saving fuel.

This change was made by a sharp application of the front brakes, flipping the bike forward over the handlebars onto the free third wheel, turning the steerable front wheel into a steerable back wheel.

At the same time the rider was required to swiftly transfer his hands onto the spare handlebars, something that was never successfully achieved without a subsequent visit to the local A&E.

The Triumph T120R Bonneville Three